HIDDEN WOMEN

The African-American Mathematicians of NASA Who Helped America Win the Space Race

by Rebecca Rissman

CONSULTANTS:

Elizabeth S.S. Smith
CAD Models and Drawings Lead,
Systems Engineering and Integration Office
in NASA's Space Station Program Office,
Johnson Space Center

Sarah Shull
Senior Systems Engineer, Mission Planning
Office, NASA's Johnson Space Center

Danielle DeVoy
Mission Integration Manager and Rehearsal
Anomaly Team Lead at Engility

CAPSTONE PRESS
a capstone imprint

Encounter books are published by Capstone Press,
1710 Roe Crest Drive, North Mankato, Minnesota 56003
www.mycapstone.com

Library of Congress Cataloging-in-Publication Data

Title: Hidden women : the African-American mathematicians of NASA who
helped America win the space race / by Rebecca Rissman.
Description: North Mankato, Minnesota : Capstone Press, c2018. | Series:
Encounter. Narrative nonfiction stories | Audience: Age 8-12. | Includes
bibliographical references and index.
Identifiers: LCCN 2017038592| ISBN 9781515799641 (hardcover) |
ISBN 9781515799634 (paperback) | ISBN 9781515799603 (eBook PDF)
Subjects: LCSH: United States. National Aeronautics and Space
Administration—Officials and employees—Biography—Juvenile literature.
| Women mathematicians—United States--Biography--Juvenile literature. |
African American women—Biography—Juvenile literature. | African American
mathematicians—Biography—Juvenile literature. | Space race—wwwJuvenile
literature.
Classification: LCC QA27.5 .R57 2018 | DDC 510.92/520973--dc23
LC record available at https://lccn.loc.gov/2017038592

Editorial Credits
Michelle Bisson, editor; Russell Griesmer, designer; Svetlana Zhurkin, media
researcher; Tori Abraham, production specialist

Photo Credits
Courtesy of Danielle DeVoy and Sea Launch, 101; Courtesy of Elizabeth S. S.
Smith, 98; Getty Images: Bettmann, 14, 49, Chip Somodevilla, 90, SSPL, 47;
NASA: cover, back cover, 1, 2, 3, 4, 8, 21, 22, 33, 39, 42, 51, 52, 56, 59, 60, 63, 68,
72, 76, 80, 82, 86, 92, 103, Courtesy of Beverly Golemba, 37, 45, Courtesy of
Charmaine Mann Vauters, 24, David C. Bowman, 89, Langley Research Center,
cover (far right), 34, 85; Newscom: Glasshouse Images, 29

Design Elements by Shutterstock

Printed and bound in the United States of America.
010763S18

TABLE OF CONTENTS

Katherine Johnson

GET THE GIRL

CHAPTER 1

Everyone was watching her.

It was a chilly morning in February 1962. Katherine Johnson glanced up from her calculations to see a crowd of anxious white men surrounding her desk. Each man was leaning forward, trying to catch a glimpse of her work. Her pencil danced across the graph paper. She jotted long strings of numbers that stretched to impossible lengths. Finally Johnson's pencil stopped. Her eyes darted across the numbers once, and then twice. With a sigh, she smiled and leaned back in her chair.

The crowd of men inside the Space Task Group office at the National Aeronautics and Space Administration (NASA) Langley Aeronautical Research Lab instantly broke up. The room erupted into a frenzy of chatter. Several men picked up their desk phones to report the news. Johnson had confirmed the numbers. That meant astronaut John Glenn would be safe to fly.

More than 850 miles away from Johnson's desk in Langley, Virginia, Glenn nervously walked across the sun-baked launch pad in Florida's Cape Canaveral.

He looked up at a towering rocket. On the very top sat a tiny metal capsule, his spaceship. Glenn was preparing to become the first American to orbit Earth. If all went well, his ship would zoom three times around the planet. It would exceed speeds of 17,000 miles per hour. That part wasn't what was bothering Glenn. He was worried about how—or if—he could get his ship back home.

Space flight was extremely precise. It relied on countless complex mathematical equations. If Glenn didn't direct his ship back down to Earth at the exact right moment, speed, and angle, he was doomed. His ship could bounce off Earth's dense atmosphere and skip out into space. Or it would land in the wrong spot. If it didn't splash down in a deep ocean, it could be crushed upon impact.

Glenn knew that NASA had used its new IBM computer to calculate the details of his flight. This room-sized machine was supposedly able to perform calculations faster and better than any human. But Glenn just didn't trust it. He was a test pilot. A man who followed his gut. Right now his gut told him he needed the best brains at NASA to confirm the numbers. He knew who he wanted to do the job: an African-American woman he'd seen in some of his preflight meetings. He didn't know her name but that didn't matter. He'd told his team: "Get the girl to check the numbers. If she says the numbers are good, I'm ready to go."

Glenn understood that his behavior might raise red flags. NASA expected him to toe the agency line. He needed to follow orders. He needed to perform his duties. And he needed to help the United States win the race to space. It was one thing for an astronaut to ask for a double check of numbers. It was another thing entirely to ask for a black woman to do the job.

Just then, Glenn looked up. Two NASA technicians were jogging across the launch pad toward him smiling

Astronaut John Glenn orbited Earth in *Friendship 7*.

broadly. Glenn knew Katherine Johnson must have done the math. Glenn laughed quietly and looked at the sky. He was going to space.

On February 20, 1962, John Glenn blasted off. He completed three Earth orbits before safely splashing down in the Atlantic Ocean. Glenn was celebrated as an American hero. He was the star of parades, parties, and countless news stories. One hundred thirty-five million people had watched his mission on TV.

Johnson wasn't invited to any parades. She was not the guest of honor at any fabulous parties. Few members of her own community in nearby Hampton, Virginia, even knew what she had done. None of this was terribly surprising to Johnson. She was an African-American human computer. She was used to being absolutely essential, but also unseen.

And yet NASA employed hundreds of female mathematicians as human computers. Some were white. Others were black. These computers performed the math that the engineers needed to build, fly, and track air- and spacecraft. Over decades of clumsy trial and error, NASA had learned to rely on these women to do its math. They were excellent mathematicians. In fact a 1942 agency memo stated that the "engineers admit themselves that the girl computers do the work more rapidly and accurately than they could." And, as an added benefit, letting the human computers do the math helped the engineers spend their time dreaming up new types of spacecraft.

Johnson never complained about being ignored. She knew she was lucky to be at NASA. And though some at NASA might not admit it, the agency was lucky to have her.

Katherine Johnson was a brilliant mathematician. She was born in 1918 and grew up in a small town in West Virginia. Most of the African-American girls at that time left school after eighth grade. Becoming a professional mathematician was a career few people in her hometown pursued. But Johnson was different. She turned her passion for numbers into a vocation.

Johnson had always focused on math. She was drawn to numbers even as a young child. "I counted everything," she recalled. "I counted the steps to the road, the steps up to church, the number of dishes and silverware I washed . . . anything that could be counted, I did."

Her parents and teachers recognized Johnson's talent. They encouraged the young girl to work hard. With their help, Johnson flew through school. She skipped grades to graduate high school at age 14. She graduated from West Virginia State College at age 18 with the highest honors. After college, she got married and had children. She then worked in one of the only careers available for educated women—she became a teacher. Johnson enjoyed teaching, but struggled to stretch her meager paycheck. When she heard about an opportunity for black mathematicians in Virginia, she jumped at the chance. After all, it promised to pay three times her teaching salary.

In 1953 Johnson was hired at NASA, then known as the National Advisory Committee for Aeronautics (NACA). Johnson could hardly contain her excitement at the chance to work full time as a mathematician. On her first day of work, she happily reported for duty in a building called West Area Computing. As soon as she walked in, she noticed something. The building was almost entirely staffed by other black people. Johnson was used to segregation. Growing up in the South, she was familiar with the notion that black and white people had to use separate facilities. Jim Crow laws, a series of rules that enforced racial segregation, had been part of her life since birth.

Johnson's supervisor was a black woman named Dorothy Vaughan. She greeted her new employee and showed her to her desk. Vaughan explained Johnson's new responsibilities. Each morning Vaughan would distribute mathematical equations to her staff of computers. When they finished, the computers would turn their work in to Vaughan. She would then return it to the correct departments. Occasionally, Vaughan explained, she might send Johnson out to a specific department to do on-site calculations.

Just two weeks after Johnson started in West Area Computing, Vaughan handed her an on-site assignment. She would be helping calculate numbers for the Flight Research Division. The engineers in this division were some of the agency's smartest. They worked on incredibly complex problems. Their math took them to the cutting edge of aeronautics.

As a black woman, Johnson at first met some resistance from her white coworkers. On her first day,

Johnson smiled at the white man working next to her. He just walked away. But she came to get along very well with her white male coworkers. They appreciated her curiosity and intelligence. Johnson loved how much they loved their jobs. She even adopted their morning ritual. She would get a cup of coffee, sit at her desk, and read through the daily newspapers and aviation journals. She scanned them for new information about advancements in the aerospace industry. Any news she spotted in the papers might affect her work. Johnson's colleagues noticed her commitment and drive. They stopping thinking about her as a "colored computer." Now they simply thought of her as "Katherine."

Johnson was delighted to have found such a challenging workplace. After years of searching, she knew she had landed in the right spot. NACA appreciated her efforts and gave her a place to thrive. But the Flight Research Division wouldn't be the end of Johnson's story. Her work there would later land her a coveted seat in the Space Task Group—the division charged with winning the space race.

African-Americans staged a sit-down strike at a lunch counter in 1960 after a store refused to serve them.

CHAPTER 2

THE SPACE RACE

Katherine Johnson wasn't the first black woman to find a bright future in the stars. Black slaves had studied the constellations for centuries. They etched the North Star into their brains. Enslaved people could follow this beacon out of the South. If they were lucky enough, they might even follow it to freedom.

Slavery had been abolished in the United States for nearly 100 years when Johnson helped send John Glenn into space. But life for black Americans was still very hard. Many white Americans held onto old beliefs. They thought that black people were inferior. Reminders of the way black people had been treated in American history were everywhere. Even the space-age campus at Langley could not escape the past. It was built on land that had once been a plantation. In fact, NACA did not officially buy the land until 1950. This means that employees at Langley spend their days on land that at one time was worked by slaves.

In the 1960s racial tensions in many parts of the country were high. Activists in the civil rights movement sought to end discrimination. They fought against segregation. Black students in cities such as Greensboro, North Carolina, engaged in peaceful sit-ins. They sat in whites-only sections of lunch counters to protest racial segregation. Their actions were often met with resistance by angry white people.

Some civil rights activists—black and white—took their fight on the road. Activists called Freedom Riders rode buses into the segregated South. Some people did not like what the riders were doing. They wanted the black riders to follow the rules of segregation. Mobs of white people attacked the Freedom Riders. The assaults were sometimes very violent.

While civil rights activists were fighting for progress, another American battle raged. This fight wasn't on the ground. It was in the sky.

The Soviet Union and the United States were the two greatest global powers. Each wanted to show that it was the best. They raced to develop new and better military firepower, technology, and economies. This fight became known as the Cold War. Each side tried to show that it was more powerful than the other. One way to show superiority was to be the first to explore outer space. The U.S. and the Soviet Union frantically sprinted to build rockets, satellites, and other spacecraft, in an effort that became known as the space race.

The Soviet Union dealt the U.S. its first blow in the space race in 1957. It launched a beachball-sized satellite into Earth's orbit. They called it *Sputnik*. This is the Russian word for traveling companion. Americans didn't think of the metal orb as a harmless companion. Many were terrified. They feared that the Soviet satellite was spying on them. Some even worried that the next Soviet space mission would be deadly. They feared a Soviet spacecraft might drop nuclear weapons on the U.S.

Two months after *Sputnik,* Americans tried to launch a satellite of their own. The rocket meant to boost the satellite into space exploded just 4 feet off the ground. The mission was a flop. American space scientists were embarrassed. The press nicknamed it "kaputnik" and "dudnik."

The U.S. responded by doubling down on its spaceflight efforts. President Dwight D. Eisenhower changed the National Advisory Committee on Aeronautics to the National Aeronautics and Space Administration in 1958. This change showed a shift in priorities. NACA had worked on new types of airplanes. NASA would continue that work, but it would also focus on spacecraft.

NASA launched a brand-new division called the Space Task Group. This group hoped to send the first Americans into space. But it couldn't do so without mathematical pros like Katherine Johnson.

When NACA transitioned to NASA, one very important change occurred. The agency desegregated. This meant that the all-black West Computing Division was abolished. The employees scattered to various divisions. In reality, the official desegregation of NASA did not have a very big impact on the way its staff interacted. Black and white employees already regularly worked together on assignments. In fact, when the agency desegregated, there were only nine black women still working in West Computing Division. All the rest of the black computers had been assigned to other divisions. Nevertheless, desegregation did not end racism at NASA. Black employees still struggled to find equal treatment and recognition regardless of the division in which they worked.

The creation of NASA centralized the nation's space program. Early space projects that had been run by the Navy or Army were transferred to NASA. The agency also received an enormous budget—about $340 million per year. NACA's annual budget had been about $100 million per year. This shift in money and resources reflected the importance of the space race.

The Soviets dominated the early years of the space

race. They first sent more satellites and then sent a dog into space. Engineers at NASA's Space Task Group set their sights on sending a man into Earth's orbit. They thought that would be better than the Soviet's accomplishments. However, they did not yet know how to do so. They needed someone to come up with the math. Katherine Johnson saw her peers working hard on the problem, and she wanted to be involved. She spoke up. "Let me do it," she told her supervisor. "Tell me where you want the man to land, and I'll tell you where to send him up." She spent a year crunching numbers, researching, and testing her findings. Finally, in 1960, she became the first woman to publish a paper at Langley's Aerospace Mechanics Division. Her paper provided the groundwork the Space Task Group needed to begin pioneering orbital flight.

But the Soviet Union beat the United States to the punch again. In April 1961 Soviet cosmonaut Yuri Gagarin became the first human to fly in space and orbit Earth. Americans were humiliated. Some at NASA were discouraged.

Yuri Gagarin circled Earth in *Vostok 1*.

Less than a month later, NASA launched astronaut Alan Shepard into space. Katherine Johnson helped to develop his trajectory. But the achievement paled in comparison to everything the Soviets had done. Shepard was only in space for 15 minutes.

President John F. Kennedy was not discouraged by the slow progress. In fact, he raised the stakes. In an address to Congress, the young president said, "I believe that this nation should commit itself to achieving the goal, before this decade is out, of landing a man on the moon and returning him safely to the Earth."

Kennedy's speech gave Americans something to feel hopeful about. He encouraged them to root for NASA, the government agency staffed by the country's best minds. All of America's dreams about space flight rested upon the shoulders of NASA employees.

NASA had chosen seven men to become the first group of astronauts. Their spacecraft was called the *Mercury*. The press called them the Mercury 7, and they soon became

The Mercury 7 astronauts quickly became among the most famous men in America.

celebrities. *Life* magazine reporters followed them around. They interviewed their wives. They even reported on their favorite meals. Americans hungrily devoured every detail about the astronauts.

Thus, the American public began a love affair with space. This space craze spread to all parts of American culture. *The Jetsons* TV show became a family favorite in 1962. This animated cartoon sitcom featured a futuristic family living in outer space. Wealthy Americans bought Cadillac cars, which had exaggerated tailfins. These projections made cars look like they could fly right off the highway and into space. Many Americans felt excited, proud, and eager to see what NASA would do next.

The mood at NASA was different. Employees there worked at a frantic pace. Their task was daunting. They wanted to get a man to the moon before the Soviets. This meant they had to develop the math and technology needed first. Nearly all Americans were watching NASA. But many NASA employees had their eyes trained on the agency's human computers. They knew that NASA couldn't get a man on the moon without them.

Miriam Mann

CHAPTER 3

RUNNING NUMBERS

Miriam Mann stared at the television set in the corner of the NASA breakroom. The tiny screen showed Scott Carpenter's space capsule zooming skyward from its Florida launch pad. The TV news anchor commented, "Today, May 24, 1962, the fourth American man will probe the depths of outer space." If all went well, Carpenter would duplicate John Glenn's flight. This would further prove to the world that NASA could safely fly men in space. As the enormous rocket painted an arcing trail of white steam through the sky, Mann sighed with relief. Soon the rocket was a tiny speck on the screen.

Satisfied that the launch had gone off without a hitch, the petite African-American mathematician got back to work. She was helping to develop the math needed to allow two spacecraft to meet while in outer space. It was called a rendezvous. This was daunting work. It was also essential. NASA engineers were toying with the idea of landing men on the moon using a system of two spaceships. One ship would orbit the moon with an astronaut inside. The other ship would carry two astronauts to the moon's surface. When the astronauts were ready to leave the moon, they would fly back into space and dock with the orbiting craft. This proposal required complex and exacting math. If the two spacecraft weren't able to rendezvous, it could be a disaster. The two astronauts in the moon lander would not have the power to get home on their own. They would float in space until they ran out of oxygen.

Mann was up to the task. She had been working at the agency for 19 years. During that time, she had developed a reputation as a talented mathematician. She spent her first years at (what was then) NACA working in West Area Computing. The building was nearly a mile from most of the agency's major research hubs, including the wind tunnels and important office buildings. Being this far away highlighted the division between African-American employees and their white peers. They were not just segregated. They were also separated by a great distance.

In some ways, though, NACA was an unusually progressive employer. The fact that the agency hired African-American female computers at all was remarkable. Their family-friendly employment policy was also unusual. They hired married women. The agency also allowed women to continue to work after they had children. Many employers at the time only hired unmarried women and fired them when they got married.

But NACA remained deeply saturated in racist ideas. For example, the job application process was harder for African-American women than it was for white women. African-American women were required to take a chemistry course before they were hired. White applicants did not need to take the course. This double standard frustrated Mann. She already had a chemistry degree from Talladega College. However, her annual salary of $2,000 at NACA was worth the frustration.

A TINY BATTLE
OF WILLS

Miriam Mann glanced over her shoulder. No one was looking. She winked at her friend Dorothy Vaughan and started toward the table in the back of the Langley cafeteria. Her heels clicked against the linoleum floor in a rapid tap-tap-tap. Vaughan groaned. She knew what was coming.

The table was featureless except for a small sign propped up in its center. Neat handwritten letters spelled out "COLORED" on the crisp white cardboard. Mann found a seat close to the sign. The pint-sized black woman stretched her arms skyward in an exaggerated yawn. Then, in a move that was supposed to look casual, she brought her arms down and knocked the sign into her lap. Mann flashed a sneaky grin at Vaughan.

Vaughan shook her head and sighed. She looked around the cafeteria. Nearly everyone else in the room was white and male. None of them seemed to have noticed Mann's theatrics. "You know your husband hates this sign-stealing business," she hissed at Mann. "He says they're going to fire you over it."

"Colored" signs separated blacks from whites in the segregated South.

Mann just shrugged as she tucked the sign into her purse. "Then they're just going to have to do it."

Miriam Mann stole dozens of "colored" signs from the Langley cafeteria between 1943 and 1958, when the agency desegregated. Each time she took a sign down, she would feel a quiet sense of accomplishment. A day or two later, another sign would pop back up. It was a tiny battle of wills. Mann kept stealing signs, and some mysterious employee kept replacing them. When NASA desegregated, the signs disappeared for good. But the feelings behind them lingered on.

There were other obstacles Mann faced that her white peers didn't have to deal with. White women at NACA could live in a dormitory on campus. This made their commute into work each day a short trip. African-American employees weren't allowed to live in the dorm. They typically moved into nearby communities like Hampton, Virginia. They then traveled the 7 miles to work by bus or carpool. Small differences like this contributed to the feelings of inequality at NACA.

Mann spent her first years helping NACA develop new military aircraft. World War II created a need for new, powerful airplanes. Countries such as Germany and Great Britain had very advanced airplanes. But the U.S. military needed new aircraft of its own. The country hurried to catch up to the technology used by other nations. It did this by pouring time, money, and brainpower into organizations such as NACA. In 1938 the American aircraft industry was the country's 41st largest industry. By 1945 it was the largest industry in the world. The U.S. was determined to become a leader in airplane technology. Mann was thrilled to help.

Those early days at NACA had been hard but exciting. The war effort was all-consuming. The human computers worked in three shifts. One shift was in the morning, one was in the afternoon, and one went through the night. This ensured that someone would be on hand to do calculations for the engineers and scientists on staff, no matter the time. Computers like Mann often worked six days a week.

Then the war ended. Many human computers assumed their jobs would end too. In other industries around the nation, women were being let go. Men returned from the war to resume their careers. Women were ushered back into their domestic roles. But NACA was different. After the war the quest for aeronautic success continued. In 1946 NACA employed about 400 female computers. And these women took on whatever mathematical tasks the agency needed.

With time, Mann's assignments shifted. She started doing work related to spacecraft flight. This change reflected the agency's focus on winning the space race. To do so, all hands were needed on deck.

Just three months after Mann watched Scott Carpenter's flight, the Soviets advanced again in the space race. They sent two manned spaceships up at the same time, in August 1962. The *Vostock 3* and *Vostock 4* were small capsules. Each held a Soviet cosmonaut. The two capsules flew close to one another as they orbited Earth. It looked to some as though the Soviets were practicing flying in formation. If that were the case, they might be running rendezvous numbers of their own.

Mann and her colleagues at NASA knew that they needed to keep working if Americans were going to be the first to the moon.

Mercury astronaut Scott Carpenter lifted off
from Cape Canaveral on May 24, 1962.

Mary Jackson

A WOMAN IN THE WIND TUNNEL

Mary Jackson peered into NASA's 4-foot wind tunnel. Part of an airplane wing was perched on a metal stand inside. It was fall 1962 and Jackson was running a few experiments on a new type of airplane wing. She walked back to a console filled with buttons and meters, and flipped a switch. A deafening blast filled the room. The wind tunnel pummeled the wing with strong blasts of air. After a few minutes, Jackson flipped the switch off and the room fell back into silence. Her ears rang as she peered inside the wind tunnel. She smiled to see the airplane wing intact.

Jackson hoped she would finish this experiment in the next few days. NASA engineers needed her to start testing a new space capsule soon. It was called *Apollo.* The cone-shaped capsule could take three men into space.

Engineers at NASA thought it might be the right craft for a moon mission. Before it could go into space, Jackson and other engineers needed to test it in wind tunnels. Doing this would ensure that the capsule could withstand the high speeds of launch and re-entry.

Mary Jackson was an unusual figure in the wind tunnel room. Most of the employees there were white men. Jackson was a 41-year-old African-American female engineer. As an engineer, she was able to design her own experiments and interpret data on her own.

Jackson hadn't started at the agency as an engineer. When she was hired in 1951, she had been a human computer. She was very qualified for the position. She had a dual degree in mathematics and physical science from Hampton Institute. This meant her education was as good if not better than that of her peers.

One day in 1953 Jackson was working with a group of white computers on the east side of Langley. After a few hours of work, she needed to use the restroom. She politely asked her white coworkers, "Can you direct me to the bathroom?" The white women cruelly laughed.

Mary Jackson (front row, right) with her coworkers

They told her they hadn't a clue where her bathroom was. Jackson clamped her jaw shut and marched out of the room.

Later on, Jackson bumped into a lead aeronautical engineer. His name was Kazimierz Czarnecki. When the white man asked about her day, Jackson exploded. She told him how angry she felt. She explained how insulting the women had been. She vented and complained. Then suddenly she remembered where she was and what her position was at the agency. She clamped her mouth shut. Czarnecki was a white man in a powerful position. She shouldn't talk to him this way. But Czarnecki wasn't upset with her. In fact, he shocked Jackson by asking, "Why don't you come work for me?"

Jackson promptly joined Czarnecki's team working on wind tunnels. Engineers used these powerful chambers to simulate the air moving over airplanes and spacecraft at high speeds. The wind tunnels helped them take very precise measurements of how the air behaved. They would then send these numbers to human computers to use in calculations. This process helped them ensure that their planes and spacecraft wouldn't fall apart mid-flight. It also helped them refine their designs to be faster.

Czarnecki hadn't known about Jackson's dual degrees when he hired her. After he discovered her qualifications and saw her work, he began giving her more challenging assignments. Most computers were not allowed to do much. They mostly just crunched

A Project Mercury capsule underwent tests in a NASA wind tunnel.

the numbers they were given. Czarnecki had Jackson doing much more. He had her firing up an immense wind tunnel herself. She was allowed to position the aircraft inside on her own. But Czarnecki wasn't done pushing Jackson. One day he suggested she become an engineer. Jackson was taken aback. The idea was thrilling. It was also scary.

Engineers at NASA had much more authority than the computers. The job promotion would be wonderful for Jackson. It offered a better title, rank, and pay. The agency even offered engineering courses at a local high school. Employees could take these courses and learn what they needed to be promoted. The system was great. NASA wanted its employees to grow and learn. There was just one problem—the high school where the engineering classes were held was segregated. This meant that Jackson wouldn't be allowed to take them.

But Jackson wasn't easily intimidated. She bravely asked the city of Hampton for permission to attend courses to become an engineer. The city allowed it. In 1956 she began taking engineering courses. In 1958 she became NASA's first black female engineer. That same year, Jackson and Czarnecki coauthored their first report on the wind tunnel findings.

In the years after becoming an engineer, Jackson accomplished amazing things. She published more research papers on her wind tunnel findings. She also became active in her community. She hosted a career panel in 1962 for black junior high school students. She paired up with a white female engineer to give a talk called the "Aspects of Engineering for Women." Jackson felt strongly that more women should work in science and engineering. She was also committed to showing black youths that they could find promising futures at NASA. The agency needed all the help it could get to win the space race.

In October 1962 an American astronaut named Wally Shirra orbited Earth for more than nine hours. It was the longest space flight yet for an American. Shirra did scientific experiments. He took photos of Earth. He also tested various ways to move his spacecraft around while in flight. The mission was a huge success. But the U.S. was still behind in the space race. The Soviets seemed to be about a full year ahead. They had flown a crewed space mission that lasted 25 hours in 1961. The cosmonaut on board that flight had also done experiments and taken photos. If the Soviets kept up this pace, they might beat the U.S. to the moon.

Gordon Cooper was the youngest of the Mercury 7 astronauts.

CHAPTER 5

TESTING ROCKETS

American astronaut Gordon Cooper completed the Mercury program in May 1963. He orbited Earth a whopping 22 times. His mission was riddled with glitches. Systems lost power. His instrument panels gave unreliable readings. A harmful gas called carbon dioxide started to build up inside his ship. Cooper stayed calm. He expertly guided his spacecraft back to Earth. Thirty-four hours after lift-off, he splashed down in the Pacific Ocean. His ship was just 4 miles away from its targeted landing spot. Cooper had survived a frightening flight and showed the world what a NASA astronaut could do.

One month after Cooper's difficult mission, the Soviets sent a woman into space for three days. Valentina Tereshkova spent her time in space doing experiments and taking photos.

Later that year Dorothy Vaughan celebrated her 20th anniversary at NASA. The agency honored the 57-year-old with a quiet ceremony. Vaughan was given a special certificate and a nickel-sized golden pin. The pin was decorated with NASA's logo and a tiny ruby. Vaughan accepted her keepsakes with pride. As an African-American female mathematician, Vaughan knew she had accomplished something extraordinary.

Vaughan wasn't the only one being celebrated that day. Her friend Miriam Mann received the same certificate and pin. The two women had started working as human computers together in 1943. While Mann had remained in her role as a computer, Vaughan had advanced. She became NACA's first African-American manager in 1949.

This position put her in charge of all the computers in West Area Computing. Each day she divided up the work between her staff of computers. She also communicated with the managers of other departments to see how her computers could help them accomplish their work. All the other managers were white. Vaughan

Dorothy Vaughan (left) with NASA coworkers

was good at her job. In her nearly 10 years as a manager, she developed friendly relationships with people all over the agency.

Vaughan knew that NACA wouldn't need its pool of human computers forever. Mechanical computing devices were becoming more common. These machines were bulky. But they could do simple computations faster than humans. Many people around NACA wondered if their jobs would be replaced one day by mechanical computers. Vaughan didn't wait around for this to happen. Instead, she learned everything she could about mechanical computers. Langley offered evening and weekend computer courses. Vaughan jumped at the chance to enroll. She also urged her black peers at NACA to do the same. She wanted to be sure that they would still be valuable to the agency in the future.

When NACA transformed into NASA in 1958, it was clear that Vaughan's preparations were on target. West Area Computing was dissolved. All the African-American women who worked in the division were sent to new job assignments. Vaughan lost her title as manager. She was reassigned to the new Analysis and Computing Division. It was an integrated division where she worked with black and white men and women.

Vaughan's new job involved working with a room-sized IBM computer. Instead of assigning math equations to a human computer, Vaughan was now programming them into a mechanical computer. She did this by feeding the computer a series of stiff, rectangular cards. Each card had been stamped with holes. The cards gave the computer directions. A single equation could require thousands of cards. If the cards were out of order or had been stamped in the wrong spots, the whole equation would be flawed. They would have to start over.

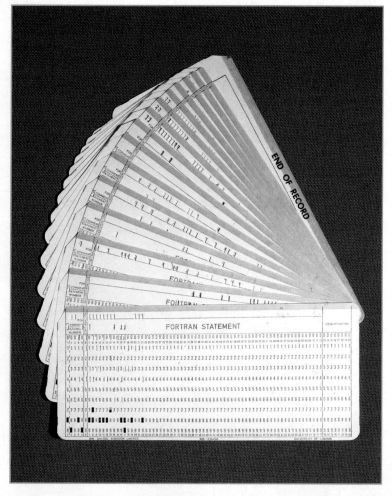

The original data-processing cards used at NASA

The work was complex and often overwhelming. It involved learning an entirely new way to work. Vaughan was entirely up for the challenge. She became an expert in FORTRAN, a computer programming language. Few of her colleagues were as fluent in the complex language. This meant that Vaughan often found herself in the position of telling her colleagues how to do their jobs. Her coworkers, many of them white men, appreciated her positive attitude and willingness to help.

Many departments within NASA used the computer. This gave Vaughan the chance to work on a wide variety of tasks. One was Project Scout, a rocket NASA hoped would help them get crewed missions into space. Vaughan helped Scout engineers with computer tasks and with on-site data collection. She drove out to the rocket's testing facility on Wallops Island, Virginia, several times as part of her job. When her children asked what she was doing on the island, Vaughan kept her lips sealed. Scout was a secret project. She followed NASA rules, even within her home.

NASA workers programming with FORTRAN

Project Scout was only a small part of NASA's race to beat the Soviets. The 76-foot-long rocket was one of many projects into which the agency was channeling energy and money. NASA leaders gave the people working on Scout an unusual amount of freedom. They were encouraged to work however they wanted in order to create a trustworthy rocket. The Scout team put in long hours. Launch days were exhausting affairs. In 1961 Vaughan and her team managed to launch a capsule containing a weighted dummy into space. It orbited Earth four times. The dummy weighed as much as an astronaut's body. Launching it showed that the rocket was strong enough to boost a human into orbit.

In the end, Scout didn't send any men to the moon. The powerful rocket was instead used to launch satellites into Earth's orbit. Scout was still considered a success. The Scout team showed that teamwork and innovation were essential to the American space program.

Vaughan strongly approved of this focus on teamwork. She had always gone out of her way to be a good team player. From her days as a manager all the way through her time as a computer programmer, Vaughan understood that the success of the agency depended on its employees working well together.

The first Scout launched in 1960 at Wallops Island, Virginia.

Annie Easley

ANNIE EASLEY AND THE CENTAUR

It was November 22, 1963. Annie Easley stood outside the launch pad in Sandusky, Ohio, listening nervously. "Three . . . two . . . one . . . ignition!" went the countdown. A giant fireball erupted below the Centaur rocket. The ground beneath Easley's feet rumbled. Slowly, the massive rocket began to lift into the air. It rose faster and faster until it zoomed up into the sky. She shouted with joy and relief. The 30-year-old African-American mathematician had been working on the problematic Centaur for a year. She was delighted to see it soar through the sky.

The Centaur was complex and dangerous. It used a new kind of fuel made from a mix of liquid hydrogen and liquid oxygen. Properly constructed, it would be one of the most powerful rockets yet designed by Americans.

Improperly constructed, it could be a deadly bomb. NASA engineers needed to turn the Centaur into a reliable rocket. Easley gladly took on the challenge.

Easley had worked at NASA's Lewis Research Center in Ohio since 1955, when she was hired as a human computer. She was one of only four African-American female professionals at Lewis. Despite this, she didn't feel like a pioneer. She simply wanted to get her job done. It helped that she enjoyed the work. She was a gifted mathematician with a knack for solving problems.

At first the only problems Easley solved were assigned to her by white male scientists and engineers. She did some calculations by hand. For others, she used the agency's large calculating machines. These beasts could do simple functions, such as adding, subtracting, and multiplying. But they were loud! She would later laugh, thinking about the sound they made: "clonk, clonk, clonk, clonk." She had been glad when the agency bought its first IBM computers. These machines had not just changed her job, they had also changed her job title. To avoid confusing the humans and the machines, the agency had started calling Easley and her peers math aides or mathematicians. This was a step in the right direction. It acknowledged their expertise and ability. But it wasn't quite enough. Many of these women wanted to advance further professionally.

The IBM computers came at just the right time. People at NASA were racing to come up with a plan for getting a man to the moon. They used the computers to perform extremely complex math. This helped them try out various ideas for rockets, spacecraft, and energy sources. Easley was fascinated by the computers. She remembered a lesson her mother had taught her: "You can be anything you want to be, but you have to work at it." Easley threw herself into learning all about computers. She and many of the other human computers taught themselves to operate the new machines. They fed the giant IBMs stacks of paper cards punched with holes. As NASA purchased more advanced IBMs, Easley learned more complex computer programs. Soon she became a confident computer programmer.

A model of a Centaur rocket was tested in a wind tunnel.

The Centaur rocket had started out as an Air Force project. Then it was adopted by NASA's Marshall Space Flight Center in Alabama. After the Centaur exploded in a disastrous launch in May 1962, the project was transferred again. This time it was sent to Lewis. When the Centaur project came to Easley's department, she was ready. She jumped into the work.

Easley used her computer skills to help speed up the work on the unreliable rocket. She knew how to use computer programming languages such as FORTRAN. She also developed new computer codes herself. This allowed her to customize her work to solve specific problems. She devoted her skills to the Centaur problem. Eventually she helped create the code needed to boost the powerful rocket off the ground. Easley also flew down to Cape Canaveral, Florida, to watch Centaur launches with her team.

At the same time, NASA launched the Gemini program. Between 1965 and 1966, the program included 10 crewed space missions. The Gemini missions helped prepare NASA for a mission to the moon. Astronauts on these flights tested new vehicles. The astronauts also did the first U.S. spacewalks, floating outside of their spaceships. Their spacesuits kept them safe from the dangers of space. The Gemini 6 and 7 missions flew at the same time and met while in orbit.

The Soviet space program appeared to slow down. Though they had achieved the first space walk in 1965, the Soviets did not send any crewed missions into space in 1966. This left Americans wondering if their Cold War opponent might be faltering. With this lag in Soviet space action, it seemed as though the Americans might be catching up. Annie Easley hoped that was the case. Her work on the Centaur proved what a group of determined mathematicians could accomplish with the right motivation. President Kennedy's goal of sending men to the moon before 1970 was a powerful incentive for everyone at NASA.

In 1966 the Centaur brought Americans one step closer to fulfilling Kennedy's request. NASA engineers combined the Centaur with another rocket called the Atlas. Together they boosted the United States' first unmanned moon lander into a successful flight. The *Surveyor 1* landed on the moon and collected valuable information. NASA then used this data to prepare for a manned moon landing.

Ed White was the first American to float in space.

Christine Darden

CHAPTER 7

A YEAR OF TRAGEDY AND NEW HOPE

Christine Darden took a break from studying in June 1967. The 24-year-old African-American mathematician stood up from her desk and looked out the window. The Virginia State College campus was lovely, even in the thick summer heat. Darden was almost done with her master's degree in applied math. It was time to think about what to do next. She had applied for teaching jobs at a few colleges, but wasn't sure she wanted to be a professor. She walked to the school's career placement office. The career counselor listened to Darden's background and exclaimed: "Gosh, I wish you had been here yesterday. NASA was here and they're hiring." Darden filled out an application a day late and sent it in, hoping the agency would take a chance on her. Darden was fascinated by space and the space race. She was hopeful that she might be able to help the country beat the Soviets in the race to the moon.

The year had been tragic for both the United States and the Soviet Union. First, on January 27, 1967, NASA had experienced a heartbreaking setback. Astronauts Ed White, Gus Grissom, and Roger Chaffee had all burned to death inside the new Apollo capsule during a rehearsal launch. Their mission was called Apollo 1.

Apollo 1 was a tragedy that tore through NASA and the nation alike. The Apollo program represented America's chance at a moon landing. Americans were counting on a victory. After the fire, NASA worked hard to understand what had gone wrong. They studied the burned capsule, and then locked it away at Langley. A plaque was placed on launch pad 34, where *Apollo 1* had burned. It read, "ad astra per aspera," Latin for "A rough road leads to the stars."

The Soviets experienced a catastrophe of their own in April 1967. Cosmonaut Vladimir Komarov was killed when his parachutes failed to open. His ship crashed to Earth. Radio controllers reported hearing

Apollo 1's command module the day after tragedy struck

Komarov screaming in rage as his ship plummeted toward the ground. The cosmonaut had been skeptical about the safety of his spacecraft. Some thought his angry screams were directed at the Soviet engineers.

He believed they had sent him into space in an unreliable craft.

The space race was risky business. Both the Americans and Soviets were working at a frantic pace to outdo one another. NASA engineers were scrambling to develop the technology needed to send men to the moon safely. To do so, the agency needed as many brilliant mathematicians as it could get.

Christine Darden was hired by NASA in the summer of 1967. She was delighted when she learned about her first job assignment. She would be in the division that was working on the re-entry calculations for the upcoming Apollo missions. This seemed like a dream come true. She was going to use her expertise to help the U.S. beat the Soviets.

Darden had studied advanced mathematical concepts in graduate school. She had also become familiar with computer programming. Darden was optimistic about using these valuable skills at NASA. But she soon realized that her job assignment wasn't at all what she wanted. She had been placed in a computing pool. She worked with a group of other women to do math for the engineers who worked down the hall. She and the other computers worked on large spreadsheets all day long. She filled in numbers and did simple computations. She wasn't able to use her extensive education to come up with new ideas. All she was allowed to do was follow directions.

Darden was part of the second generation of African-American women at NASA. She had been just 1 year old when Dorothy Vaughan started work at the agency. Darden had been in high school when *Sputnik* looped around the planet. She had been in graduate school during the Gemini program. Darden knew that just 10 years earlier, NASA had still been segregated. The fact that women like Mary Jackson were now working as aeronautical engineers was astounding. But Darden was not satisfied with her job. She wanted more for herself.

During her first years at NASA, Darden became close with some of the original West Area Computing workers. They were much older than Darden, but they offered her support and guidance. She befriended Katherine Johnson. The two sang together in their church choir and attended social events together. They played cards with friends and talked about life. Johnson encouraged Darden to keep working. Sometimes Johnson visited schools to tell them about jobs at NASA. Whenever she was at a school, Johnson always mentioned her very smart friend Christine.

Although she was frustrated, Darden kept working at NASA. Before long she learned that she had the same educational background as the engineers who worked just down the hall from her.

Darden became angry. One day, she went to her supervisor. "Can I transfer to an engineering area?" she asked. The answer was a sharp "no." Her supervisor told her it would be impossible.

Darden then asked if she could go to graduate school. She wondered if an additional graduate degree might help her get a promotion. Her supervisor told her, "No, we don't think you can do that." Darden knew of white employees for whom NASA had paid for graduate school. She quietly fumed.

When the first successful Apollo launch happened in October 1968, Darden pushed her frustrations aside. She felt hopeful for the astronauts inside the *Apollo 7* capsule as they orbited Earth. The 10-day mission was a triumph. The new Apollo capsule performed well. Two months later, another mission launched.

Apollo 8 orbited the moon. This was the first time humans had ever orbited another body in space. Darden could hardly believe she worked for the agency that made it possible.

Maybe, she thought, the U.S. might win this space race after all.

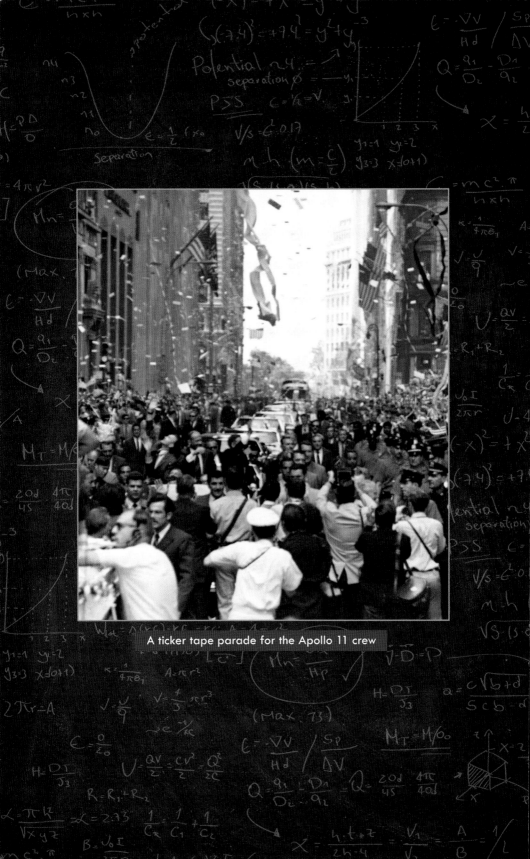

A ticker tape parade for the Apollo 11 crew

THE MOON LANDING, A DREAM COME TRUE

A group of black women dressed in pink and green crowded into the cramped lobby of the Hillside Inn. The hotel in the Pocono Mountains was the site of the Alpha Kappa Alpha (AKA) sorority leadership conference. AKA sisters came from around the country to talk about opportunities to help their communities. Katherine Johnson was one of the leaders of the meeting. She had remained active in AKA long after her college days were over. She had been looking forward to this weekend for a long time. She had planned to talk about scholarships, community improvement, and literacy programs. And she had also planned to do as much catching up as she could. She loved these women. But the socializing had been preempted by the space race. It was July 20, 1969, and NASA was about to land two men on the moon.

The small TV was tuned to the CBS newscast. News anchor Walter Cronkite was excitedly narrating the action. A lunar lander called the *Eagle* was slowly descending toward the moon's surface. As it got closer, Cronkite struggled to remain composed. He chuckled nervously and wiped sweat from his forehead.

The mood in the hotel lobby was also hopeful and excited. Johnson knew how important this mission was. She had worked for years developing, testing, and double-checking the math needed to get the Apollo capsule into space, orbiting the moon, and back safely. She had personally helped calculate the trajectory for this mission.

Johnson also knew how easily the mission could become a disaster. If any of her numbers were off, the astronauts were as good as dead. Luckily for the crew, Johnson said, "I had done the calculations and knew they were correct."

Johnson was confident in her own part of the flight, but the team in mission control remained nervous. If anything at all went wrong with the moon landing, the astronauts could be stranded or killed. When the lunar lander thumped down onto the moon's powdery surface, astronaut Neil Armstrong calmly said into his radio: "The *Eagle* has landed." Mission control erupted into hoots and cheers. They radioed back, joking about the tension: "You got a bunch of guys about to turn blue, we're breathing again."

At 10:56 p.m. Eastern Daylight Time, Armstrong stepped onto the moon. He said, "That's one small step for a man, one giant leap for mankind." Buzz Aldrin soon followed. Together they explored what Aldrin described as the "magnificent desolation" of the moon's surface.

Before climbing back into the lunar lander, Aldrin and Armstrong planted an American flag on the moon. There was no wind on the moon, which meant the flag would hang limp. NASA had anticipated this. They gave the astronauts a thin aluminum frame to hold the flag aloft. The simple structure kept the stars and stripes proudly on display. Many people thought that this flag ended the space race. Americans had beaten the Soviets to the moon. The crisp flag proved it.

The AKA sorority sisters watched the television footage quietly. Some held their hands over their mouths in disbelief. Walter Cronkite summarized what many of them were feeling. "For thousands of years

Buzz Aldrin's bootprint on the moon

now, it's been man's dream to walk on the moon. Right now, after seeing it happen, knowing that it happened, it still seems like a dream. And it is, I guess—a dream come true."

Finally the rocky, frustrating, and sometimes tragic race to the moon was over. The Soviets had achieved incredible things in space, including sending the first artificial satellite into Earth's orbit. They also sent the first dog, man, and woman into space. The Soviets were the first to spend a day in orbit, and the first to fly a long-duration space flight. They were also the first to perform a spacewalk. But for many Americans, these accomplishments paled in comparison to Armstrong's walk through the chalky moon dust.

After 21 hours and 36 minutes, it was time to leave. The *Eagle* lifted off the surface of the moon. As the moon fell away below them, Aldrin looked out the window. He watched as the exhaust gases from the lander knocked the American flag flat.

The Apollo 11 crew safely splashed down off the coast of Hawaii on July 24. They had finally fulfilled

President Kennedy's challenge to land a man safely on the moon and return him home. Inside mission control, men lit cigars and waved American flags in celebration.

Later the members of the crew were honored at several epic "splashdown" parties. In Los Angeles, 1,440 guests—including President Richard Nixon and Vice President Spiro Agnew—celebrated the crew at a lavish gala. They were served individual moon-themed ice cream desserts. Each came with its own miniature American flag.

There were no parades for Katherine Johnson, Dorothy Vaughan, Miriam Mann, Mary Jackson, Annie Easley, Christine Darden, or any of the other human computers. There were no extravagant balls either. While the Apollo astronauts mingled with celebrities and global leaders, the black women at NASA went about their work as diligently as ever.

Of all the former computers, Johnson received the most public attention for her work. After John Glenn's historic flight, her story appeared in local newspapers.

An African-American newspaper, the *Pittsburgh Courier,* ran an article about her in 1962, calling her a "Mother, wife, career woman!" Articles like this helped her become a familiar figure within black engineering and science networks. Despite this modest fame, Johnson remained humble about her role at NASA. Even friends like Christine Darden weren't quite sure what Johnson had done to help win the space race.

The work performed by Johnson and others behind the scenes was crucial to the success enjoyed by the crew of Apollo 11. In an interview years later, Armstrong credited the work of the nameless "hundreds of thousands" who helped get him to the moon. Armstrong knew that the staffers at NASA were working as hard as they could to achieve success in space.

For many at NASA, Apollo 11 was not the end of the space race, but the start of something new. Armstrong said it was the "beginning of a new age." Victories like the moon landing were cause for celebration, but not for rest. There were new accomplishments to achieve and new frontiers to explore.

Inside the *Apollo 13* lunar module

"HOUSTON, WE'VE HAD A PROBLEM"

In the years leading up to the moon landing, Katherine Johnson coauthored two unique papers. One proposed that astronauts flying to Mars could navigate using the stars, moons, and planets visible out their spaceship window. The other suggested that, in an emergency, an astronaut on a moon mission could use visible stars to find a safe course back to Earth without the use of onboard computer navigation. Few could have predicted how important these papers would become.

Four months after Apollo 11's success, NASA landed the crew of Apollo 12 on the moon. In April 1970 the agency launched Apollo 13. It was hoping for yet another moon landing. But then, after nearly 56 hours of flight, disaster struck.

Apollo 13 commander Jim Lovell heard a loud bang.

His ship lurched. Alarms started to sound inside the ship. Lovell spoke calmly into his radio: "Uh, Houston, we've had a problem."

Mission control burst into action. Men frantically rushed to learn what had caused the bang and alarms. Soon things onboard *Apollo 13* got even worse. The ship's power and oxygen supplies began to fall. Lovell and his crew would later learn that an oxygen tank had exploded. The blast caused devastating damage to the ship.

The astronauts scrambled to stay alive. Their original mission was called off. They would not land on the moon. Instead they needed to use all of their remaining power to return to Earth. Mission control instructed them to turn off most of the ship's computers. They hoped this would save enough of the ship's power to get the astronauts home alive. Without their onboard computer systems, they could not rely on electronic navigation. This meant they needed to find a new way to get home.

Luckily, Katherine Johnson had provided just such a strategy in her papers. Lovell turned to Johnson's idea to try to save his crew. He squinted out the small windows and strained to see the stars. He was well versed in astronomy. His NASA training taught him to recognize dozens of stars. All he needed was a clear view of his surroundings. Then he could use Johnson's ideas to align his spacecraft correctly. Once he faced it the right way, he could fire the engines and start the long trek home. But all Lovell could see out the windows was debris. The explosion had kicked up a cloud of dust and shards of metal. They surrounded the ship. The oxygen leaking out into space had frozen into tiny crystals, which also hovered nearby. This meant Lovell couldn't see any stars.

Lovell tried various tactics to get a clear view of stars. He rolled his ship from side to side. He tried facing different directions. Nothing worked. In the end, the ship's commander was forced to abandon Johnson's navigational proposal in favor of other backup plans. One of the ways he did this was by lining up his spaceship with Earth's terminator. This is the line that separates daylight from shadow on Earth. This helped him bring his limping ship and crew back safely to Earth.

The Apollo 13 astronauts safely landed in the South Pacific Ocean.

The fact that Johnson's work ultimately did not bring home the Apollo astronauts did not make her work on navigation methods any less important. NASA trusted her ideas enough to try to use them in one of the agency's greatest emergencies.

In one of the darkest moments of the Apollo 13 mission, Commander Lovell turned to the lunar module pilot, Fred Haise. "Freddo," he said, "I'm afraid this is going to be the last moon mission in a long time." Lovell's prediction was wrong.

Apollo 13 was not the last mission to the moon. Apollo 13 became known as NASA's "successful failure." It showed what the greatest scientific minds in America were capable of. Between 1971 and 1972, four more Apollo missions landed on the moon.

Following the success of the Apollo program, the Soviets quietly gave up on their effort to land a human on the moon. Instead they shifted their work to other areas of space science. They worked on building space labs. Later the Soviets focused on the International Space Station.

And so, the great space race was over. The work done at NASA fulfilled the dreams of countless Americans who eagerly followed its progress and cheered its successes. But NASA made other dreams come true as well. When the agency spread its wide net, looking for talent that could advance its efforts toward space travel, it scooped up people who might otherwise have been overlooked. These unexpected and often unappreciated talents were given the chance to show just how brilliant they really were.

Katherine Johnson (right) with NASA coworkers in 1970

CHAPTER 10

AFTER THE RACE

None of the early black female mathematicians at NASA walked on the moon. They didn't orbit Earth. None flew short space missions. But their contributions to the space race were beyond measure. Without the work accomplished by these women and their peers, NASA may never have made such enormous aerospace strides in such a short amount of time. Neil Armstrong's first steps on the moon were not his alone. Rather, the footprints he left in the fine moon dust were those of countless hardworking women and men at NASA.

In the years after the moon landing, the lives of the women at NASA took different paths. Each woman's career trajectory was as unique as her personality. Miriam Mann did not live to see the success of Apollo 11. Poor health caused her to retire from the agency in 1966. The following year, she died. Her family has worked to remember her legacy. Her granddaughter, Duchess (Miriam) Harris, wrote a book about the human computers in 2016.

Dorothy Vaughan ultimately grew frustrated with the agency. After nearly 10 years as NACA's first black supervisor, Vaughan was demoted in 1958 when the agency became NASA. She had been an excellent manager and a brilliant computer programmer, but NASA never again rewarded her work with a promotion. Finally, in 1971, she retired after 28 years at the agency.

Vaughan wasn't alone in her struggle to advance. After Mary Jackson became the first black female engineer at the agency, she was incredibly productive. She authored or coauthored some 12 research papers for NASA. Her work mostly focused on the way that air behaves around airplanes. This was detailed, complex research. Jackson was good at her job. But her initial growth at the agency slowed. By the mid-1970s, she felt the same frustrations that Vaughan had. She

Mary Jackson at work

wanted to advance professionally. She did not think NASA wanted to promote female professionals as readily as males. In 1979 Jackson did something bold. She left her engineering role and transferred to become Langley's federal women's program manager. This job change was a demotion. Jackson took the lower-level job in order to make a difference for female employees in the future. She also worked as the Affirmative Action program manager. These roles gave her the chance to improve the working conditions of women and people of color at NASA. Jackson retired from NASA in 1985.

Annie Easley never worked at Langley. She remained at the Lewis Research Center in Ohio for her entire career. This geographic difference didn't

Annie Easley worked on complex equations.

prevent her from experiencing some of the same issues as Vaughan and Jackson. In the 1960s Easley wanted to go back to school to learn more about mathematics. Her white peers had done so with financial aid from NASA. Easley tried to get financial aid of her own. Her requests were denied. This did not stop her. Easley was determined. She paid for her own schooling and juggled night classes with work. When school became too consuming, she took an unpaid three-month leave from NASA. This was frustrating because Easley knew of others who had been paid to take leave for school. Finally, in 1977, she earned her bachelor of science degree in mathematics. In the late 1970s, NASA paid for some specialized courses that she needed. Easley stayed on at NASA until 1989. Toward the end of her career, she became an advocate for people of color at the agency. She became an equal employment officer. This role helped her to address discrimination at NASA.

Christine Darden started at NASA more than 10 years after Mann, Johnson, Vaughan, Jackson, and Easley began their careers. This meant that she was able to avoid some of the obstacles they faced as black mathematicians. In the years after the first moon walk, Darden was promoted to aerospace engineer. She later became the technical leader of a group working on sonic booms. She enjoyed several further significant promotions. In 1999 she became the director of the Program Management Office of the Aerospace Performing Center at Langley. She has published nearly 60 research papers. NASA awarded Darden 10 certificates of outstanding performance for her work. She has also been recognized by various scientific and philanthropic organizations for being a leader in her field. Darden recognizes that her career was heavily influenced by the pioneering efforts of the first black women at NASA. She said, "I was able to stand on the shoulders of those women who came before me, and women who came after me were able to stand on mine."

Katherine Johnson's career at NASA wasn't the longest, but it may be the best remembered. In recent years her story has been featured in documentaries,

Christine Darden (top left) and Katherine Johnson (seated left) at a lecture

books, and a feature film called *Hidden Figures.* Her fame is well deserved. Over her 33 years at the agency, she accomplished amazing things. She coauthored 26 research reports. She also worked on the space shuttle and Earth resources satellite projects. In looking back on her career, she said that she was most proud of the work she did on the Apollo project. She helped devise the math needed to help the lunar lander rendezvous with the command module in space. This was groundbreaking technology that required extremely complex math.

Johnson loved being able to contribute to it. Her career at NASA was not easy. She was forced to work hard, not only to do her job, but also to overcome the discrimination she faced as a black woman. None of

President Barack Obama presented Katherine Johnson with the Presidential Medal of Freedom.

this changed her affection for her work. She later said, "I loved going to work every single day." When she was 97 years old, Johnson was awarded the highest civilian honor—the Presidential Medal of Freedom. President Barack Obama gave her the award. He said that she "was a pioneer who broke the barriers of race and gender, showing generations of young people that everyone can excel in math and science, and reach for the stars."

The story of the first black mathematicians at NASA is not over yet. Those who've died continue to shape the narrative of black history through their legacies. Their children, grandchildren, and great-grandchildren will tell their stories and remember their work. Those that are still alive revive their histories with each speech and awards ceremony they attend. Many people today find strength in the work these women accomplished in the past.

Sarah Shull

EPILOGUE

NASA operates out of 10 major facilities in the United States. NASA's current goals are much broader than they used to be. At its outset NASA focused on winning the space race. Today people at NASA are involved in a wide range of tasks. NASA's vision is to "reach for new heights and reveal the unknown for the benefit of humankind." These new heights include developing the technologies needed to send humans to Mars. They also include possible missions to asteroids and other places in space. NASA continues to work on the International Space Station. This is an international space project that hopes to show how humans can survive in space for long periods of time.

Sarah Shull is a NASA senior systems engineer. She works in the Mission Planning Office at NASA's

Johnson Space Center. Shull does not feel that her gender has been an obstacle in her career at NASA. She has found the agency to be an inclusive employer. Her story shows that NASA has made progress in becoming a more diverse workplace. In 2016 NASA reported that 22.5 percent of its engineers were women. Nationally, women only make up about 11 percent of engineers.

Shull has worked for NASA in a variety of roles, including flight controller in mission control. Getting this job was very difficult. People who want to work in mission control must pass a challenging test. It subjects them to various simulations. Some include simulated disasters or emergencies on space missions. Shull had to show that she knew exactly how to respond to keep her crew safe. The phrase Annie Easley's mother used to tell her, "You can be anything you want to be, but you have to work at it," resonates with Shull. She often tells children that they can absolutely go into a career in space science. But she warns them that it will be difficult: "You're not picking the easiest path in life. School is going to be hard. You're going to feel like you're working a lot harder than your friends, but it's worth it in the end."

In its early days, mission control was staffed entirely by men. Shull reports that her time in mission control was very different. About one third of the people in the room were women.

In 2010 Shull experienced one of the highlights of her career. She sat at the flight controller desk in mission control and watched as the first SpaceX commercial cargo demonstration flight succeeded. She remembers watching the astronauts on the space station grasp the ship with a robotic arm. She felt incredibly proud to have been a part of it. This accomplishment ushered in a new phase of space travel. Shull knew that it meant that space travel would begin to expand.

In the past it had been limited to government and government-funded projects. Now commercial companies were involved. They could do things in space that NASA and other space agencies might not prioritize. And it meant that more people would get the chance to travel into space. This expansion of the industry is very exciting for Shull. She says it "has the potential to decrease the cost [of space travel] and open the opportunity to more folks. And that's an awesome thing."

NASA released information about its employees in 2016. The agency employed minority engineers at the same rate or higher than the national average. The only exception to this was in their Asian or Pacific Islander workforce. That group represented a slightly lower percentage than the relevant civilian workforce. This information shows that NASA has done considerable work in improving its diversity. It also shows that the agency could still improve.

Elizabeth S.S. Smith is a systems engineer. She has worked at NASA's Johnson Space Center for more than 35 years. Her experiences with racial bias reflect the agency's growth and its shortcomings.

She recalls her first days at NASA with mixed emotions. She says she was blessed to work in a field she loved. She also appreciated her team. Her managers supported her work and recognized her skills. But Smith's first years at NASA were not all good. She experienced many incidents of racism.

In the early 1980s, Smith worked with a team of white male engineers. They produced digital drawings of the plans for the International Space Station, called computer aided designs (CAD). The space station hadn't been built yet. Each day teams around NASA held brainstorming meetings. People in these meetings would come up with ideas for the space station. After every meeting, Smith and her team would re-create their CAD models to reflect the new ideas. This was a lot of work. It was time-consuming. Smith and her team had to wait until a meeting finished to learn what they needed to change. Soon Smith's supervisor decided to have her team attend these meetings. This would save time. It would also help them know exactly what to change in their models.

When Smith started attending the meetings,

Elizabeth S.S. Smith

she noticed something. She was the only African-American woman in the room. She could feel that some people did not want her there. But she continued to attend the meetings. She needed to stay up to date on the space station.

Soon someone called Smith's division manager. They told him Smith couldn't come to any more meetings. Smith fondly remembers hearing her boss's response through his closed office door. He shouted: "She's going to the meetings. She's going to continue to go. And you can't stop her!" Smith was relieved. Her boss stood up for what was right. He defended his employee, regardless of her race or gender.

Another woman with a unique perspective on NASA is Danielle DeVoy. She has worked for various groups that have contracted with the agency. Today she works at an engineering consulting firm. DeVoy has two roles in her current position. She is a mission integration manager and a rehearsal anomaly team lead. As a rehearsal anomaly lead, she stages rocket launch rehearsals for the Air Force. She deliberately causes problems for the launch team. She then watches as the team solves the problems. After each rehearsal DeVoy judges whether the team is prepared enough for launch. She says, "I'm like the quarterback to the whole day of launch countdown."

DeVoy's field is still mostly male. She often calculates the percentage of women in her meetings. She notes that it is usually between 10 and 20 percent. Despite this, DeVoy usually does not feel as though she is treated differently because she is a woman. If anyone does treat DeVoy inappropriately, she is quick to address the issue. She hopes that her willingness to speak out will encourage more people to do the same.

DeVoy's career has provided her with amazing opportunities, including that of working alongside America's first female astronaut, Sally Ride. DeVoy's interactions with Ride shaped her outlook on being a woman in the space industry. DeVoy knew that Ride's career had been hard. Ride had been forced to deal with reluctant flight instructors who didn't believe women should be astronauts. She politely handled pesky interviewers who shouted questions like "Do you wish you were a boy?" And she experienced teachers who told her she was wasting her time studying science.

Today DeVoy remembers Ride's difficult career when she interacts with other women in the field. She always tries to reach out and lend a helping hand whenever she can. DeVoy hopes to inspire and assist women in a way that Ride, as a pioneer, could not benefit from in her own career.

Danielle DeVoy

DeVoy encourages young women in the industry to hold themselves to a high standard. She reminds them not to second guess their roles or responsibilities, especially if they are the only women in the room.

The women working at and with NASA today are on their own personal journeys. Their goals and dreams are as individual as they are. Sometimes the paths they take are difficult. Sexism and racism can still make their lives difficult. But just as the women who came before them did, they will persevere. And the women who follow in their footsteps can look back and feel proud of how far they have come.

Sally Ride

TIMELINE

March 3, 1915 The National Advisory Committee on Aeronautics (NACA) is formed during World War I

1943 NACA hires its first group of black human computers, including Miriam Mann and Dorothy Vaughan

1949 Dorothy Vaughan becomes NACA's first black supervisor

1950 NACA purchases land from the Chesterville plantation in Virginia for its Langley site

1951 Mary Jackson is hired as a human computer at Langley

1953 Katherine Johnson is hired as a human computer at Langley

1955 Annie Easley is hired as a human computer at Lewis

October 4, 1957 The Soviets launch *Sputnik*, the first artificial satellite to orbit Earth

1958 NACA becomes the National Aeronautics and Space Administration (NASA). The agency officially desegregates. Mary Jackson becomes NASA's first black female engineer and coauthors her first research report

April 12, 1961 Soviet cosmonaut Yuri Gagarin becomes the first human to fly in space and orbit Earth

May 5, 1961 Alan Shepard becomes the first American to fly in space

May 25, 1961 President John F. Kennedy challenges Americans to land a man on the moon and bring him safely home before the end of the decade

February 20, 1962 John Glenn becomes the first American to orbit Earth. Days before his launch, Katherine Johnson confirms his flight trajectory by manual calculations

June 16, 1962   Soviet cosmonaut Valentina Tereshkova becomes the first woman in space

November 27, 1963   The Centaur rocket is paired with the Atlas booster and successfully launches. Annie Easley contributes to the software needed for the project

1966   Miriam Mann retires from NASA

1967   Christine Darden becomes a human computer at Langley

January 27, 1967   The crew of *Apollo 1* is killed in a preflight fire

July 20, 1969   Neil Armstrong is the first man to walk on the moon

April 13, 1970   An oxygen tank onboard *Apollo 13* explodes. The crew then attempts to use Johnson's ideas for navigation by stars to get home

1971   Dorothy Vaughan retires from NASA

1977   Annie Easley earns her bachelor of science degree in mathematics

1979   Mary Jackson becomes Langley's federal women's program manager

1983   Christine Darden earns a PhD in mechanical engineering

1985   Mary Jackson retires from NASA

1989   Annie Easley retires from NASA

Christine Darden becomes the technical leader of NASA's Sonic Boom Group of the Vehicle Integration Branch of the High Speed Research Program

November 24, 2015   Katherine Johnson receives the Presidential Medal of Freedom

GLOSSARY

aeronautic—relating to aircraft

Cold War—the name for the period of hostility between the United States and the Soviets that lasted from 1945 to 1990

cosmonaut—Russian astronaut

FORTRAN—type of computer programming language. FORTRAN stands for "formula translation"

Jim Crow—laws and rules that segregated black people in the United States

plantation—large farm that is cultivated by resident labor. In the American South, many plantations were worked by slaves

satellite—object that moves around a planet or other cosmic body

segregation—practice of separating people of different races, income classes, or ethnic groups

sit-ins—type of protest used during the civil rights movement. Protesters would sit in a whites-only area, such as a lunch counter, and refuse to leave

trajectory—path followed by a flying object

READ MORE

Feldman, Thea. *You Should Meet: Katherine Johnson.* New York: Simon & Schuster, 2017.

Harris, Duchess, and Sue Bradford Edwards. *Hidden Human Computers: The Black Women of NASA.* Hidden Heroes Series. Minneapolis, Minn.: Essential Library, 2016.

Holt, Nathalia. *Rise of the Rocket Girls: The Women Who Propelled Us from Missiles to Moon to Mars.* New York: Little, Brown, 2016.

Shetterly, Margot Lee. *Hidden Figures* Young Readers' Edition. New York: Harper Collins, 2016.

INTERNET SITES

Use FactHound to find Internet sites related to this book.

Visit *www.facthound.com*

Just type in 9781515799641 and go.

CRITICAL THINKING QUESTIONS

1. Miriam Mann made a habit of stealing the "Colored" sign out of the Langley cafeteria. What are some examples of ways that the other black human computers rebelled against social and cultural constraints?

2. What happened in the 1960s that contributed to an environment in which black women could find work at NASA? How was NASA a positive employer for women? How was working at NASA difficult for women?

3. Why did black women at NASA feel that they had to "follow the rules"? Has this changed over time?

BIBLIOGRAPHY

Conger, Cristen. "Did NASA Win the Space Race?" HowStuffworks.com. 2 May 2017. http://science.howstuffworks.com/nasa-space-race1.htm

"History." NASA.gov. 25 April 2017. 3 May 2017. https://crgis.ndc. NASA.gov/historic/Human_Computers

"Human Computers at NASA." Macalester.edu. 9 May 2017. http://omeka.macalester.edu/humancomputerproject/map

"July 20, 1969: One Giant Leap for Mankind." NASA.gov. 14 July 2014. 20 May 2017. https://www.nasa.gov/mission_pages/apollo/apollo11.html

"Mercury Crewed Flights Summary." NASA.gov. 20 November 2006. 8 May 2017. https://www.nasa.gov/mission_pages/mercury/missions/manned_flights.html

Shetterly, Margot Lee. *Hidden Figures: The American Dream and the Untold Story of the Black Women Mathematicians Who Helped Win the Space Race.* New York: Harper Collins, 2016.

Smith, Yvette. "Katherine Johnson: The Girl Who Loved to Count." NASA. gov. 17 Jan. 2017. 2 May 2017. https://www.nasa.gov/feature/katherine-johnson-the-girl-who-loved-to-count

SOURCE NOTES

CHAPTER 1:

page 7, "Get the girl to check the numbers..." Margot Lee Shetterly (2016). *Hidden Figures*. New York: William Morrow, p. 217.

page 9, "The engineers admit themselves..." Joe Atkinson. (March 27, 2014). From Computers to Leaders: Women at NASA Langley. Retrieved 2 July 2017 from https://www.nasa.gov/larc/from-computers-to-leaders-women-at-nasa-langley

page 10, "I counted everything..." Katherine Johnson. (November 24, 2015). Katherine Johnson: The Girl Who Loved to Count. Retrieved 10 June 2017 from https://www.nasa.gov/feature/katherine-johnson-the-girl-who-loved-to-count

CHAPTER 2:

page 20, "Let me do it..." Margot Lee Shetterley (2016). *Hidden Figures*. New York: William Morrow, p. 190.

page 21, "I believe that this nation should..." John F. Kennedy (May 25, 1961). May 25, 1961: JFK's Moon Shot Speech to Congress. Retrieved June 10 from https://www.space.com/11772-president-kennedy-historic-speech-moon-space.html

CHAPTER 4:

page 36, "Can you direct me..." Margot Lee Shetterley (2016). *Hidden Figures*. New York: William Morrow, p. 108.

page 38, "Why don't you come..." Margot Lee Shetterley (2016). *Hidden Figures*. New York: William Morrow, p. 110.

CHAPTER 6:

page 54, "Clonk, clonk..." Annie Easley (August 21, 2001). NASA Headquarters Oral History Project. Retrieved 8 June 2017 from https://www.jsc.nasa.gov/history/oral_histories/NASA_HQ/Herstory/EasleyAJ/EasleyAJ_8-21-01.htm

page 55, "You can be anything..." Annie Easley (August 21, 2001). NASA Headquarters Oral History Project. Retrieved 8 June 2017 from https://www.jsc.nasa.gov/history/oral_histories/NASA_HQ/Herstory/EasleyAJ/EasleyAJ_8-21-01.htm

CHAPTER 7:

page 61, "Gosh, I wish you had been..." Christine Darden (2011). Christine Darden. Retrieved 20 June 2017 from https://www.youtube.com/watch?v=z_Qil_HESWY

page 66, "Can I transfer to an engineering..." Brian McNeill (April 8, 2017). Christine Darden, Featured in 'Hidden Figures,' Talks Sonic Booms and Her Career at NASA. Retrieved 25 June 2017 from https://news.vcu.edu/article/Christine_Darden_featured_in_Hidden_Figures_talks_sonic_booms

CHAPTER 8:

page 70, "I had done the calculations..." Katherine Johnson (November 24, 2015). Katherine Johnson: The Girl Who Loved to Count. Retrieved 10 June 2017 from https://www.nasa.gov/feature/katherine-johnson-the-girl-who-loved-to-count

page 71, "You got a bunch of guys..." Charlie Duke (July 20, 1069). On the Moon. Retrieved 4 May 2017 from http://apollo11.spacelog.org/page/04:06:46:06/

page 71, "That's one small step..." Neil Armstrong (July 20, 1969). July 20, 1969: One Small Leap for Mankind. Retrieved 20 June 2017 from https://www.nasa.gov/mission_pages/apollo/apollo11.html

pages 72-73, "For thousands of years now..." Walter Cronkite (July 20, 1969). Relive Apollo 11 With Walter Cronkite. Retrieved June 15 from https://www.youtube.com/watch?v=5F6B1U77dgs

page, 75, "Mother, Wife..." Margot Lee Shetterly (2016). *Hidden Figures*. New York: William Morrow, p. 125.

page 75, "hundreds of thousands..." Neil Armstrong (2001). NASA Johnson Space Center Oral History Project. Retrieved 20 June 2017 from https://www.nasa.gov/sites/default/files/62281main_armstrong_oralhistory.pdf

page 75, "beginning of a new age..." Neil Armstrong (August 12, 1969). Apollo 11 Post Flight Press Conference. Retrieved June 29 from https://www.youtube.com/watch?v=XeAGGpRYmKY

CHAPTER 9:

page 78, "Uh, Houston, we've had a problem..." Jim Lovell. Detailed Chronology of Events Surrounding the Apollo 13 Accident. Retrieved 20 May 2017 from https://history.nasa.gov/Timeline/apollo13chron.html

page 80, "Freddo, I'm afraid..." Jim Lovell and Jeffrey Kluger. (1994). Apollo 13. New York: Houghton Mifflin, p. 204.

CHAPTER 10:

page 88, "I was able to stand..." Denise Lineberry (March 29, 2013). Standing on the Shoulders of a Computer. Retrieved 1 June 2017 from https://www.nasa.gov/centers/langley/news/researchernews/rn_CDarden.html

page 91, "I loved going to work..." Margot Lee Shetterly (2016). Katherine Johnson Biography. Retrieved 1 June 2017 from https://www.nasa.gov/content/katherine-johnson-biography

page 91, "a pioneer who broke the barriers..." Barack Obama (2015). Remarks by the president at Medal of Freedom Ceremony. Retrieved 20 June 2017 from https://obamawhitehouse.archives.gov/the-press-office/2015/11/24/remarks-president-medal-freedom-ceremony

EPILOGUE:

page 93, "reach for new heights..." (2016). What Does NASA Do? Retrieved 1 June 2017 from https://www.nasa.gov/about/highlights/what_does_nasa_do.html

page 94, "You can be anything..." Annie Easley (August 21, 2001). NASA Headquarters Oral History Project. Retrieved 8 June 2017 from https://www.jsc.nasa.gov/history/oral_histories/NASA_HQ/Herstory/EasleyAJ/EasleyAJ_8-21-01.htm

pages 94-95, "You're not picking the easiest path..." Sarah Shull (April 20, 2017). Personal Interview.

page 96, "has the potential to decrease the cost..." Sarah Shull (April 20, 2017). Personal Interview.

page 98, "She's going to the meetings..." Elizabeth Smith (April 20, 2017). Personal Interview.

page 99, "I'm like the quarterback..." Danielle DeVoy (April 20, 2017). Personal Interview.

page 100, "Do you wish..." Lynn Sherr (2015). Sally Ride: America's First Woman in Space. New York: Simon and Schuster, p. 149.

INDEX

ABOUT THE AUTHOR

Rebecca Rissman is an award-winning nonfiction author of more than 300 books. Her work has been praised by School Library Journal, Booklist, Creative Child Magazine, and Learning magazine. Rissman especially enjoys writing about American history, aeronautics, and women. She lives in Chicago, Illinois, with her husband and two daughters.